COOL STUFF to COLLECT

Stephanie Turnbull

SAUNDERS
BOOK COMPANY

Published by Saunders Book Company
27 Stewart Road, Collingwood, ON Canada L9Y 4M7

With thanks to Mim Waller

Library of Congress Cataloging-in-Publication Data

Turnbull, Stephanie.
 Cool stuff to collect / Stephanie Turnbull.
    pages cm. -- (Cool stuff)
 Includes index.
 ISBN 978-1-77092-221-1 (paperback)
 1. Collectors and collecting--Juvenile literature. I. Title.
 AM231.T87 2015
 790.1'32--dc23

                          2014002623

CIP record is available from Library and Archives Canada

Photo acknowledgements
t = top, b = bottom, l = left, r = right, c = center
page 1 windu, 2-3 Zhukov Oleg; 4t OtnaYdur, c Elnur;
5c MARGRIT HIRSCH, b Africa Studio; 6tl Lubava, tc tehcheesiong,
b Birute Vijeikiene; 7 Suslik1983; 8t Louella938/all Shutterstock,
b Mim Waller; 9c Liufuyu/Thinkstock, b MARGRIT HIRSCH/
Shutterstock, 10 and 11 Mim Waller; 12l Dancing Fish/
Shutterstock, r Mim Waller; 13 Mim Waller; 14tr Madlen/
Shutterstock; c Mim Waller, b photokup/Shutterstock; 155
and c Mim Waller, b zhu difeng; 16t Sergey Novikov/both
Shutterstock; 17 Mim Waller; 18t Birute Vijeikiene/Shutterstock, b
Mim Waller; 19 Mim Waller; 20 Ljupco Smokovski/Shutterstock;
21 Mim Waller; 22t Shebeko, tl F. JIMENEZ MECA, b Mim Waller,
23, 24, 25t Mim Waller, b Africa Studio;
26t Roman Pyshchyk/both Shutterstock, b Mim Waller;
27t Mim Waller, b kuleczka; 28t keantian/both Shutterstock,
r Mim Waller, b Chimpinski; 29t mark higgins/Shutterstock,
b Mim Waller; 3ot LooksLikeLisa, b Birute Vijeikiene;
31 SisterF/all Shutterstock
lightbulb in Cool Ideas boxes Designs Stock/Shutterstock
Cover background Daboost, pencil erasers Quayside, cube
photosync, soldier and lips Crepesoles/all Shutterstock

Printed in China

DAD0058
032014
9 8 7 6 5 4 3 2 1

Contents

Cool Collections

Building a collection can be great fun! It can brighten up your bedroom, keep you busy on a rainy day, and involve your friends, too.

Get Personal

Collecting isn't about keeping everything you've ever owned and never throwing anything out! It's about selecting things that make you happy, whether they're souvenirs from vacations, presents from friends, or memories of fun times. It's a way of showing what makes you YOU.

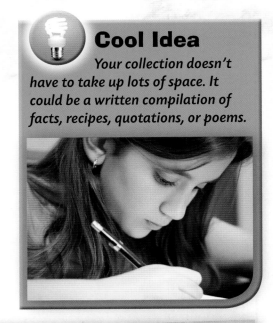

Cool Idea

Your collection doesn't have to take up lots of space. It could be a written compilation of facts, recipes, quotations, or poems.

*Many collections contain **antiques** and other precious, treasured objects.*

All Kinds of Collections

Some people buy objects that are created to be collected, known as collectibles. These might be dolls or **figurines**, **first editions** of books, or special coins. Big collections can become valuable over time, especially if they are kept in their original packaging.

Rare or very old toys can be valuable–but they aren't designed to be played with!

Other people love to collect things that aren't valuable at all, such as ring pulls, candy wrappers, rocks, or stickers from bananas! They might make displays or just keep them around to give visitors something to talk about...

Did You Know?

Stamp collecting is one of the most popular hobbies in the world. It began in 1840 when the first-ever stamps were issued. Very rare stamps sell for thousands of dollars.

What to Collect

So what should you collect? Key rings, badges, or comic books? Snow globes, marbles, or wind-up toys? It can be hard to know what to choose! Here are some handy hints to help you.

Pick a Passion

Never start collecting something you aren't passionate about—you'll soon get bored. If you're excited about cars, you could collect models of your favorite types. If you love dogs, a collection of dog ornaments, photos, and books might be fun. If vacations are what you like best, how about collecting souvenirs from places you visit?

What you collect may depend on how much space you have to store it in.

Did You Know?

Some of the most expensive things to collect are pieces of art. In 2011, a painting by the artist Paul Cézanne sold for more than $240 million.

Sort Your Stuff

It's worth checking to see if you already have items to start a collection. Perhaps you've been given several piggy banks, comic books, or trading cards as gifts. Dig things out of cupboards and drawers, and put them together. Then you can work on building your collection!

Piggy banks are ideal to collect as they come in all kinds of shapes and sizes.

Choose a Theme

Any collection is more interesting if it has a theme. Rather than collecting all stuffed animals, why not focus on a particular type, size, or style? Perhaps the theme could be a certain material—such as items made from glass, wood, or brass—or even your favorite color. Use your imagination!

Cool Idea

No space in your bedroom? Why not collect something you can store outside, such as wind chimes or garden ornaments?

Colored collections can look stylish against a plain background.

Grow Your Collection

Here are some clever ideas for how to make your collection grow. It doesn't have to be enormous—small, carefully-chosen collections can be more interesting than huge, messy ones.

Cool Idea

If you and your friends collect the same things, swap duplicates and help each other. You could pool your collections to create one really big one.

Go Shopping

Thrift stores are perfect places to find all kinds of odds and ends, and they're often cheap, too. Garage sales are also worth checking out.

You may find treasure among piles of junk!

Shop carefully—be aware that items labeled "vintage" are often expensive.

Ask for Help

Make sure family and friends know what you're collecting, so they can check their cupboards for you or buy useful items as birthday presents. Elderly relatives may have fascinating old postcards, photos, books, or coins that are ideal for your collection.

Money Matters

Don't get carried away when you're buying stuff–it could costing a fortune!
If an item is expensive, think hard about whether you really need it. You might be better off saving your money or perhaps buying several cheaper items for the same price.

Old letters and postcards may be fragile, so always look after them carefully.

Did You Know?

One man in the US has collected 2,388 pairs of sneakers, while a man from Germany owns an amazing 600 toasters. A woman in the UK has collected 5,000 bars of soap!

Keep Track

Make a list of items in your collection, so you don't end up losing or forgetting some. Why not take photos of each one, so you can remind yourself of what you have while shopping and avoid buying duplicates?

Smart Storage

Store your collection neatly and safely. This will ensure that items don't get damaged or lost and make your precious things look special. Why not clean your room to create some space?

What to Avoid

Don't try to cram your entire collection onto one shelf. It will look cluttered, and you may knock over or break items as you reach for them. It's also tricky to keep dust-free! Beware of storing things on windowsills, too, as sunlight will fade them over time.

The more space you have, the easier it will be to see everything and keep it clean.

Display cabinets like this are perfect for showcasing lots of items.

Some collections, such as cacti, need to be on a sunny windowsill.

Great Displays

Arrange pottery, clocks, figurines, and big objects over several shelves. Position the largest ones at the back so you can see everything, and use **shelf organizer** to add extra layers.

Shelf organizer

Stackable storage bins don't take up much room and let you see everything easily.

Big jars and vases are great for filling with small objects such as shells, toy cars, or marbles to create displays.

Cool Idea

How about using a tiered cake stand to store lots of small objects, such as thimbles, rocks, or paperweights?

Super Storage

If you don't have room to keep your collection on display, choose interesting containers to store things in. See if you can find old jewelry boxes, suitcases, or cookie tins. Thrift stores are full of unusual tins, boxes, and holders.

Did You Know?

Bob Bretall, from California, owns the world's largest collection of comic books. His comics are stored in boxes and stacked all over his house. He keeps a detailed list and knows exactly where to find each one!

Hanging Collections

If you don't have much shelf space or room for boxes, collect objects to hang on your wall or dangle from a stand. Here are some stylish suggestions for hanging up your stuff.

Wall Art

Instead of putting photos or postcards in boxes or albums, mount them in frames and ask an adult to put picture hooks on your wall. Arrange frames in a neat, interlocking design to create an artsy wall display that can spread as your collection grows.

Handy Hooks

Single hooks or rows of coat hooks are perfect for hanging a collection of keys, medals, bags, or key rings. Look for unusual hooks to make your display extra cool, and don't forget that you can hang more than one object on each hook.

Pick a style of hook that fits your wall.

Mix frames of different colors, shapes, and sizes to make your collection look more varied.

Cool Idea

Why not string wool, ribbon, or even white lights around your room and use clothespins to attach cards, ticket stubs, and other lightweight objects? You could decorate plain wooden clothespins with felt pens, glitter, or stickers.

Push-Pin Hangers

One alternative to making lots of holes in your wall is to use a cork board and tacks as hangers. For extra impact, cover your board in fabric, stretching it tightly and tacking it at the back.

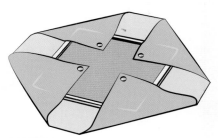

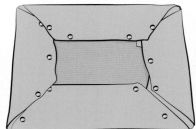

Add a length of ribbon to hang your board on a door knob or picture hook.

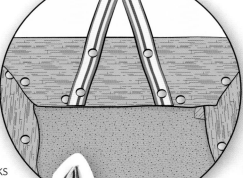

Stylish Stands

A mug tree makes a simple stand for a hanging collection. Make it look special by painting it with **acrylic paints**, covering it with stickers, or winding ribbon around it.

Arrange colorful tacks or pushpins across the front.

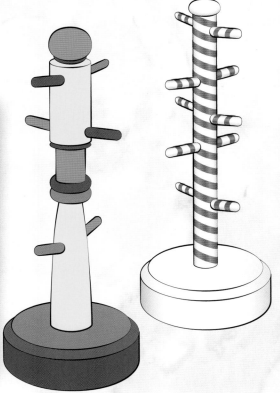

Fantastic Photos

Photos don't take up much space and remind you of events, places, and people you love. Here are some great tips for arranging, storing, and displaying your photo collection.

Photo Themes

Decide what kind of photos interest you. Do you want a reminder of vacations or would you rather collect snapshots of pets, buildings, or flowers? Perhaps you could use photos of relatives to make a family tree, or maybe you prefer photos that make you laugh!

*Try covering a wall or large cork board with a colorful **montage** of your favorite photos.*

Did You Know?

Digital photo frames store hundreds of photos. Scroll through them for a slide show!

Start Snapping

Collecting photos is a good reason to keep a camera or cell phone handy and take lots of pictures. Download them regularly so you don't risk losing them. Be selective–choose just the best images to print and display.

Cool Idea

Try cutting photos into interesting shapes or snipping off boring backgrounds.

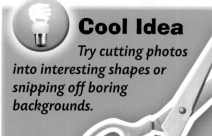

Be Organized

Write the date and other information on the back of your photos and store them flat, so they don't crease. Photo albums are perfect for keeping your collection in order. Add captions or labels, so you know what's what.

Awesome Albums

Why not make your own photo album? These expandable albums can be as big as you like, and you can personalize them with stickers or drawings.

1. *Find a large sheet of thin cardstock and mark out as many equally-sized rectangles as you can, each big enough to hold a photo.*

2. *Cut along the long edge and fold the panels accordian-style, like this.*

3. *Make more strips in the same way and tape the ends together to make one long piece.*

The number of strips you add depends on how many photos you want to put in.

4. *Cut two pieces of thicker cardstock just bigger than your folded piece. Glue to the end panels to make a cover.*

5. *Glue a strip of ribbon across the back cover so you can tie your album shut. Now add photos!*

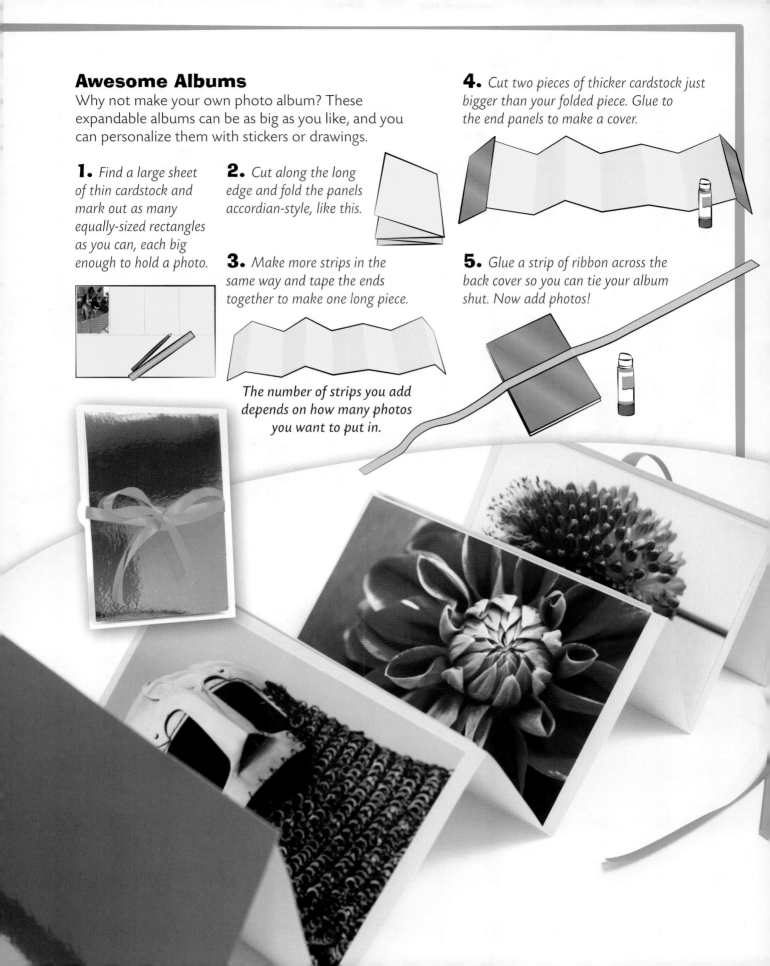

Scrapbooks and Displays

If you keep photos of special memories or people, you may want to include extras such as ticket stubs, letters, postcards, and newspaper clippings. Here are some ways to make your collection stand out.

Perfect Pages

Scrapbooks are ideal for displaying your stuff, but you need to plan each page if you want them to look good. Try out different arrangements before you stick anything down.

First, give your page a heading and select a few photos and extras to go on it. Choose a big, striking photo as the central image and place other elements around it. You can overlap things or place them at angles. Don't cram in too much!

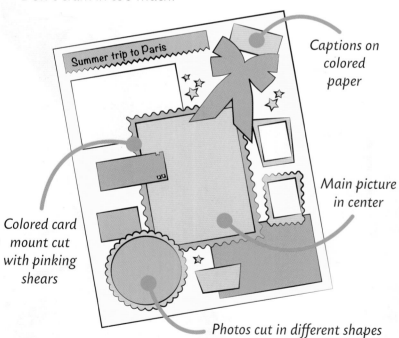

Summer trip to Paris

Captions on colored paper

Main picture in center

Colored card mount cut with pinking shears

Photos cut in different shapes

Borders or colorful card **mounts** can make images stand out. Use **pinking shears** to make wavy edges, and remember that you can **crop** photos with scissors. Add captions if you need them, either printed or written by hand.

Cool Idea

Use your imagination when creating scrapbooks. How about adding stickers, glitter, or pieces of fabric, or making a border out of cut or torn paper strips?

Creative Displays

If you don't want to fill a scrapbook, how about making one page and framing it? Another neat display idea is to cover a cork board in fabric (see page 13) and pin criss-crossing lengths of ribbon over it. Slide photos, ticket stubs, letters, postcards, envelopes, and other mementoes under the ribbon to keep them in place.

This display method prevents delicate items from being damaged with glue or pins, and you can change things whenever you want.

Did You Know?

*Scrapbooking experts buy all kinds of extra decorations called **embellishments**. They also use special hole punches and cutters to create complicated cut-outs.*

Buttons and Beads

Small things such as buttons and beads make fantastic collections. They're colorful, easy-to-find and come in all shapes and sizes. Read on to find out how to turn your collection into gorgeous displays.

Lots of buttons sorted into rainbow shades make an eye-catching display.

Super Strings

Beads and buttons have handy holes, so it's easy to string them on thread, yarn, or thin ribbon and hang them in your bedroom as long, colorful garlands. Another idea is to thread shorter lengths and tie them to key rings to make cool key chains.

Cool Idea

Store buttons and beads in empty chocolate box or egg carton compartments, or fill spice jars and keep them in a rack!

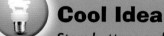

Start Sorting

You can keep all your buttons or beads in one big box, but they may get jumbled if you have a lot. Try sorting them into colors, sizes, shapes, or materials (for example metal, plastic, and fabric) and putting them in separate jars or smaller boxes.

Buttons on Display

Serious button collectors attach their buttons to special mats, using wire. You could use a piece of thick, folded cardstock. Choose your buttons, and thread a needle with thick thread.

Carefully push the needle up through the card, out of one of the buttonholes, then down again. Cut the thread and tie the two ends together.

If there are four holes, go in and out diagonally to make an "x" shape.

Colorful Collages

One of the most creative ways of showing off your button or bead collection is to sew it to fabric as part of a **collage**. **Felt** is great, as it's easy to sew on and doesn't **fray**.

1. *Mark out a shape–such as your initial–using pins. Thread a needle with brightly-colored thread and tie a knot at the end.*

2. *Sew on a few big buttons or beads and remove the pins.*

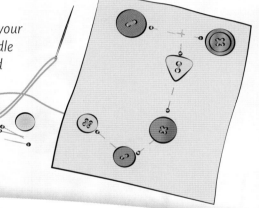

3. *Now fill in the gaps with smaller buttons or beads. When you've finished, tie a knot in the end of the thread on the back of the felt.*

Did You Know?

*Many button experts collect beautiful Victorian **enamel** buttons, which can be very expensive.*

Magnets and More

Beads aren't the only small, colorful items you can collect. Many people collect magnets, fabric buttons, sew-on patches, thimbles, vintage brooches or gemstones, and much, much more.

Fun Fabric Buttons

Fabric buttons come in a huge variety of shapes, sizes, and designs. Display them on your coat or bag, or pin them on a spare pillow. Another stylish idea is to make your own display cushions.

1. *Find an old, colorful T-shirt, or buy one cheaply from a thrift store. Using thread of the same color, carefully stitch up the bottom of the T-shirt. Stitch up the arm holes in the same way.*

*Sew along the existing **seams** to hide your stitches.*

2. *Fill the T-shirt with pillow stuffing or soft material such as old socks or towels. Push the stuffing into the corners.*

3. *Sew up the neck hole, and pin on your fabric buttons.*

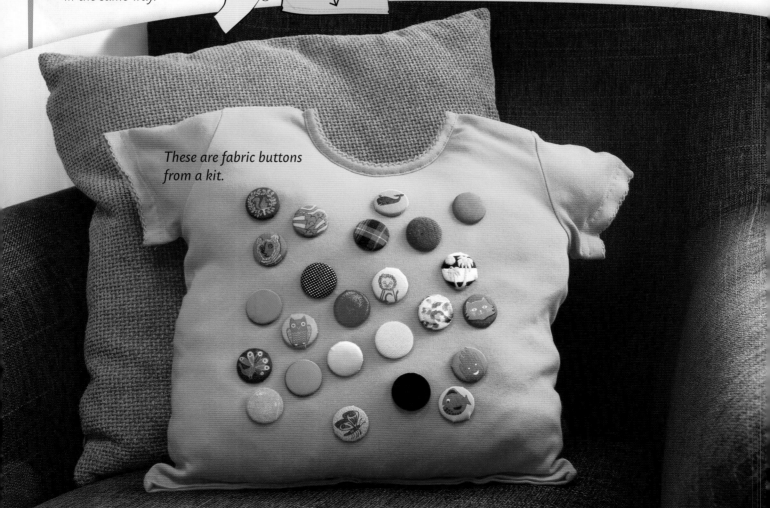

These are fabric buttons from a kit.

Making More

Need more magnets or badges? Extend your collection by making a few extras! Buy a set of small, plain magnets and put stickers on top, or use **PVA glue** to add pebbles, buttons, and other small objects.

Did You Know?

The world record for the largest fridge magnet collection is held by Louise Greenfarb from Las Vegas. She has 35,000 different magnets—and no two are the same!

To make a badge quickly, cut shapes from felt and fix a safety pin to the back.

Marvelous Magnets

Souvenir shops always sell fridge magnets, which will remind you of your vacation. If you want to display them in your bedroom rather than on the fridge, find or buy a metal baking tray and arrange your magnets on it.

Prop it up on a shelf or, if it has holes at the ends, thread yarn or ribbon through the holes and hang it up.

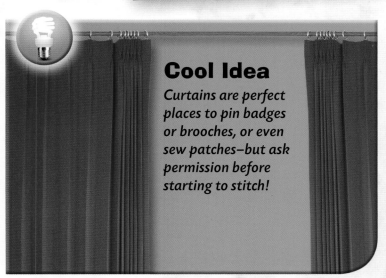

Cool Idea

Curtains are perfect places to pin badges or brooches, or even sew patches—but ask permission before starting to stitch!

Pens and Pencils

Why not collect pens or pencils? They could be vacation souvenirs, antique pens, glitter markers, or pencils with novelty tops or decorations. You can display them or have some fun and use them!

Pen Cups

The easiest way to store pens and pencils is in cups. Choose cheerful designs that liven up your bedroom, or use bright mugs, vases, or differently shaped glass jars. If you have lots of pens or pencils, sort them according to style, color, or size.

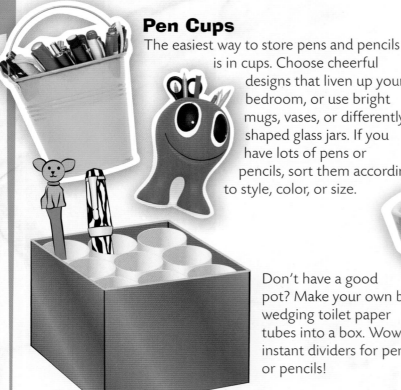

Don't have a good pot? Make your own by wedging toilet paper tubes into a box. Wow—instant dividers for pens or pencils!

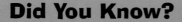

Cool Idea

*Why not store pens and pencils in **terracotta** plant pots? Paint them first with acrylic paint, or stick on shells, beads, or plastic gems.*

Did You Know?

The most expensive pens in the world are studded with diamonds and cost thousands of dollars.

Cool Containers

You may want to hide precious pens in a pencil case or other container so that no one borrows or damages them. Try using a desk drawer organizer, or buy a plastic cutlery drawer divider.

Fabric Rolls

Here's an easy-to-make fabric pen holder. Each pen has its own slot, and the holder rolls up to keep them safe.

1. *Fold a large rectangle of felt to make a pocket. Pin the edges together.*

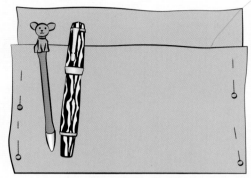

Lay your pens on top to make sure they will fit in.

2. *Use brightly-colored thread to stitch along the edges, taking out the pins as you go. Finish each line of stitching with a knot inside the pocket.*

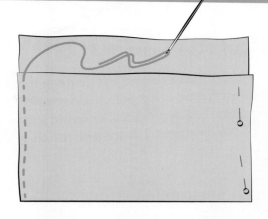

3. *Divide the pocket into roughly equal sections and mark them with pins.*

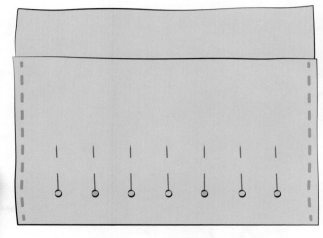

4. *Stitch along each line, through both layers of felt.*

Keep your pen holder rolled up, by tying a piece of ribbon, yarn or cord around it.

Desk Delights

You can also collect other desk items. Look for novelty pencil sharpeners, decorated rulers, funny erasers, unusual scissors, or pads of sticky notes...there's so much to choose from!

Be Selective

Avoid overcrowding by picking a theme for your collection, for example animals or vehicles. Find as many items as you can featuring that theme.

Did You Know?

There is a whole museum of pencil sharpeners in Ohio!

How about starting an ocean-themed collection of erasers and pencil sharpeners?

Cool Clips

Collections of bright metal or plastic paper clips can be attached to curtains and folders, made into long hanging chains, or even turned into colorful collages.

Cool Idea

Use stackable plastic sandwich boxes to store small things such as erasers. Choose clear boxes so you can see what's inside.

Bright Bands

Collect rubber bands and see how big a ball you can make. Or, turn them into a long chain. Here's a neat way of linking them together.

1. *Squeeze your first rubber band into a loop, like this.*

2. *Fix it in place by wrapping a second looped band up and over it...*

... and pulling one end through the other to make a knot.

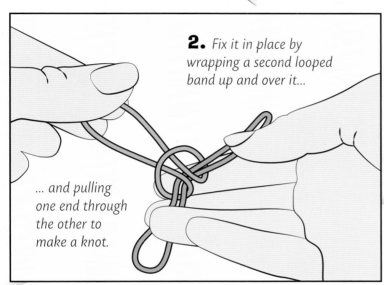

3. *Now squeeze another band into a loop and feed it through the ends of the first loop.*

4. *Feed another looped band through the ends of the loop as in step 3. Repeat until your chain is really long. Finish by wrapping and tying a final band around it as in step 2.*

These chains are especially effective if you use several bands to form each link of the chain. Experiment with bands of different lengths and thicknesses.

Books and Magazines

If you love to read, books are the perfect thing to collect. Search for everything your favorite author has written, look for books on a topic that really interests you, or track down every title in a series you enjoy.

Did You Know?

The actor Johnny Depp is an avid collector of rare books that were written by his favorite authors.

Think Creatively

For a special book collection, try hunting for books signed by authors, or look in thrift stores and antique markets for very old books. You could even collect books for their beautiful covers rather than what they contain.

On Display

Books are best displayed on a shelf, arranged by author, topic, size, or color. Keep them in place with book ends or heavy items. To display the front covers of your favorite books, try making book stands from shoe boxes.

1. *Draw a line down the middle of each long side of the box.*

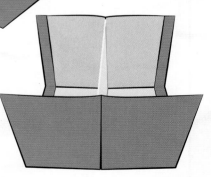

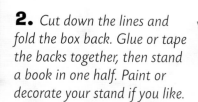

2. *Cut down the lines and fold the box back. Glue or tape the backs together, then stand a book in one half. Paint or decorate your stand if you like.*

Magazines and Comics

If magazines or comic books are more your style, store them in a box or magazine rack to avoid tearing the edges. Piles of magazines can take up a lot of space, so consider cutting out favorite pages and framing them for your wall.

Fabric racks like this one hold a lot of magazines.

Cool Idea

How about collecting maps, bookmarks, funny comic strips, or even newspapers published on your birthday each year?

Holders and Hangers

To make a simple magazine holder, find an old cereal box and use a ruler to draw a line across one of the sides, about 4 inches (10 cm) up. Draw a diagonal line up to both top corners of the box.

Cut along the lines, and remove the flap from the top of the packet. Paint or decorate your holder to make it look stylish.

You can also take a wire coat hanger and carefully bend it into a boomerang shape.

Hang it on a door knob to hold magazines or comics. Wind colorful pipe cleaners or yarn over the wire to decorate the hanger.

Nature Collections

Collecting nature items like stones, shells, leaves, and acorns won't cost you a penny! But don't leave your natural treasures in a box—have some fun making things with them.

Drying and Pressing

Cut flowers and leaves don't stay fresh for long, but they last for years if you dry them. Lay them flat on a sheet of newspaper or a few paper towels. Cover with more paper, and sandwich the whole thing between heavy books.

The newspaper or paper towel absorbs the moisture, preserving your flowers and leaves.

After a few weeks, remove your flattened flowers and leaves. Carefully stick them to a sheet of paper with tiny dabs of glue, then frame them under glass.

Pine-Cone People

Turn pine cones, nuts, and acorns into characters to liven up your room! You need some PVA glue and a few craft supplies such as googly eyes, colored card, felt, mini pompoms, or pipe cleaners.

Use your imagination to create cute animals or funny people.

Shells can be glued together to make interesting shapes or glued down onto cardboard to form a textured collage.

Did You Know?

Many craft experts skillfully weave containers from grasses, twigs, and vines, or even create whole sculptures.

This delicate grasshopper is made from coconut leaves.

Cool Idea
Take photos of your best nature finds to keep after they have faded or shriveled!

Glossary

acrylic paints
Fast-drying paints that can be mixed with water or used straight from the tube. Be careful, as they won't wash off clothes when dry!

antique
An object that is very old, beautiful, and well-made.

collage
A collection of materials, artistically arranged and glued down.

crop
To trim a photograph so that only the most important or striking section remains.

embellishments
Small decorations, such as shiny stickers, lengths of ribbon, and fabric buttons, used in scrapbooks to make pages look more special.

enamel
A colored, glassy substance that is applied to a metal surface and allowed to harden to form a smooth coating.

felt
Soft fabric that has been pressed and matted together. It comes in lots of bright colors and is very easy to cut and sew.

figurine
A small carved or molded figure.

first edition
A book from the very first printing of a title. First editions of certain books may be valuable because there are not many left, or because they are different from later editions.

fray
To unravel into loose threads at the edges.

montage
A display made up of lots of small pictures or photographs.

mount
A piece of cardstock on which a photo is fixed to display it. The mount should be just bigger than the photo and in a color that helps the photo stand out clearly.

pinking shears
Scissors with blades that are serrated, like a saw, so they cut in a zigzag pattern.

PVA glue
A strong, water-based glue, also known as white craft glue. PVA stands for polyvinyl acetate, which is a rubbery plastic substance.

seam
The line where two pieces of fabric have been sewn together.

shelf organizer
A small shelf or stand that gives you an extra surface to store objects. It stands on top of existing, larger shelves.

terracotta
Hard, orange-brown clay, often made into plant pots.

Websites

Collectibles: A-Z
http://collectibles.about.com/od/morecollectiblecategories/u/CollectiblesA-Z.htm
Check out this huge A-Z list of pretty much everything you could ever collect!

Photography for Kids
www.clickitupanotch.com/2012/07/photography-for-kids
Improve your photo collection with useful hints and tips for taking great pictures.

Scrapbooking Ideas and Keepsake Crafts
www.spoonful.com/create/scrapbooking-ideas-keepsakes-gallery
Browse lots of creative scrapbooking and storage ideas.

How to Make Paper Desk Organizers
http://tlc.howstuffworks.com/family/paper-desk-organizers.htm
Try making simple desk organizers for all kinds of stationery collections.

Index

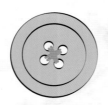